SLAVERY

"To be a slave. To be owned by another person, as a car, house, or table is owned. To live as a piece of property that could be sold—a child sold from its mother, a wife from her husband. To be considered not human, but a thing that plowed the fields, cut the wood, cooked the food, nursed another's child; a thing whose sole function was determined by the one who owned you.

"To be a slave. To know despite the suffering and deprivation, that you were human, more human than he who said you were not human. To know joy, laughter, sorrow, and tears and yet be considered only the equal of a table. To be a slave was to be a human being under conditions in which that humanity was denied. They were not slaves. They were people. Their condition was slavery."

— Julius Lester

BY JAMES MEADOWS

Published by The Child's World®
1980 Lookout Drive, Mankato, MN 56003-1705
800-599-READ • www.childsworld.com

CONTENT CONSULTANT
Kira Duke, Education Coordinator
National Civil Rights Museum

PHOTOS
Cover and page 4: Henry P. Moore/Library of
Congress, Prints and Photographs Division
Interior: Benjamin F. Powelson/Library of Congress, Prints and Photographs
Division: 20; Everett Collection/Newscom: 19; Everett Collection/Shutterstock.
com: 8, 25, 29 (right); Ken Welsh/Newscom: 13; Library of Congress, Prints and
Photographs Division: 22, 31; Liljenquist Family Collection/Library of Congress,
Prints and Photographs Division: 16; Morphart Creation/Shutterstock.com: 11;
National Portrait Gallery, Smithsonian Institute: 24, 29 (left); North Wind Picture
Archives: 5, 6, 9, 10, 12, 14, 15, 21, 23, 27, 28; Schomburg Center for Research in
Black Culture, Photographs and Prints Division, The New York Public Library: 7

LIBRARY OF CONGRESS CATALOGING-IN-PUBLICATION DATA
ISBN 9781503853744 (Reinforced Library Binding)
ISBN 9781503854055 (Portable Document Format)
ISBN 9781503854178 (Online Multi-user eBook)
LCCN: 2020943578

Printed in the United States of America

Cover and page 4 caption:
Enslaved workers in
South Carolina planting
sweet potatoes in 1862.

CONTENTS

Chapter One

THE BEGINNING

The first slave ships set sail from
Europe around 1450, more than 500
years ago. They sailed to Africa from
the country of Portugal. At the time,
Portugal was one of the wealthiest,
most powerful nations in Europe.
Even so, land owners and farmers
in Portugal wanted to be even
more rich and powerful. Portuguese
slave traders captured Africans and
forced them back to Europe.

American settlers
look on as captured
African people arrive in
Jamestown in 1619.

    Soon, other Europeans, as
well as Arab slave traders from
North Africa, became active in the slave trade. They took people
from central Africa to sell not only in Europe but also in Eastern
lands such as Arabia and India. Beginning in 1619, slave traders
captured and shipped Africans across the Atlantic Ocean to the
North America. Once there, the enslaved Africans were sold like
livestock. They were forced to work on farms, clean houses, or do
anything else their enslavers wanted. They worked long hours for
no pay. If they refused to work, they could be beaten or killed.

People captured in Africa are marched to the coast to be sold into slavery.

A different type of slavery existed in Africa before the Europeans entered the slave trade. When African tribes were at war, captured soldiers often became enslaved. These captives sometimes became part of their new culture rather than remaining slaves. They often married into the new tribe. Sometimes slaves even rose to positions of leadership and power.

European slave traders made a huge profit by selling human beings into **bondage**. The slave ships sailed south from Europe toward West Africa. Some Africans were blacksmiths or miners. Others were farmers, priests, and politicians. They were leaders and warriors, parents and children. Millions of African people were torn from their families, their homes, their land, and their goods to be sold as property.

Although slavery ended almost 150 years ago, learning about it today helps us understand the roots of the **racism** and **prejudice** that still exist. We can learn about the reasons for slavery in hopes that we can prevent similar abuse of people from happening again. And we can try to understand and defend the values of freedom and equality that the United States is founded on.

Africa is the second largest continent on Earth. It features two of the world's largest deserts, endless plains, and miles of rain forest. Africa's people are as diverse as their land. They speak hundreds of different languages. Tribes and clans often have very different religious traditions and customs. When slave traders first arrived, Africans had a difficult time banding together to fight back because their languages and customs often were so different.

This illustration shows enslaved children huddling together for comfort.

Once captured, most Africans remained enslaved their entire lives. Their children were born into slavery as well. Soon after slavery reached North America, lawmakers made it illegal for slaves to learn to read. Although many enslaved Africans had lifelong partners and families, they could not legally marry.

At the time, most Europeans believed that Africans were savages who lacked intelligence and needed whites to guide them. This was how the Europeans justified slavery. History tells a different story about African cultures. Many Africans lived in large, wealthy kingdoms such as Ghana, Mali, and Songhai.

When European slave traders captured new slaves in Africa, other Africans often helped them. Some African clans helped the slave traders capture their enemies. Europeans also bribed Africans with cloth, guns, and other forms of wealth. Later, Africans helped the slave traders to avoid being sold into slavery themselves.

The slave trade changed the entire African region. European slave traders captured thousands of Africa's strongest, most capable people. The captives were shipped to the other side of the world, year after year, for hundreds of years.

Why did Europeans create such a brutal trade? In the 1490s and early 1500s, European explorers sailed across the Atlantic looking for a faster, cheaper way to the Asian lands of India and China. Instead, the explorers found themselves on the continents known today as North and South America.

Europeans claimed the vast lands of this New World, which was already home to millions of Native Americans, each nation with its own culture. As the Europeans took the land from the local tribes and nations, they wanted cheap labor to grow crops, build towns, and provide goods and services.

A husband is torn from his wife and child as they are separated and sold into slavery.

First, they tried enslaving Native American peoples. However, many Native Americans were hunters more than farmers. They were not well suited to the work. A vast number died from **inhumane** treatment or from diseases the Europeans brought with them. Those who survived knew the land well enough to escape, and sometimes they fought back.

When enslaving Native Americans proved too difficult, the Europeans brought in captured and enslaved Africans. Many of the newly enslaved people had been farmers in Africa and had farming skills. They already had been exposed to many of the diseases the

Colonists force a Native American into slavery in the 1600s.

Europeans brought from the Old World. And enslaved Africans were less likely to escape because they did not know the lands of their new home. They had nowhere to go.

Chapter Two

SLAVERY IN NORTH AMERICA

Africans captured inland in Africa were sometimes forced to march hundreds of miles to the coast. During this exhausting journey, they were tied at the hands and neck. They marched all day long and into the evening, stopping only for a little food and water. Those who could not keep up were beaten or left to die.

Once the captives reached the coast, they were loaded onto slave ships. The more captured Africans each ship carried, the more money the slave traders made.

This deck plan of a slave ship shows how captured people were arranged as cargo.

10

The voyage across the Atlantic Ocean to North America, often called the Middle Passage, was long and cruel. The captives were chained to the deck for days at a time. They were packed in shoulder to shoulder and hip to hip.

Enslaved men being chained and sent below deck on a slave ship.

Forced to lie in their own waste and vomit, they fell victim to deadly diseases such as smallpox. Due to the awful conditions, one-third of the captives never survived the trip. Some died by jumping overboard to escape the misery.

The first enslaved Africans landed in North America in 1619. These first Africans were indentured servants. This meant that they worked for seven to ten years before being freed. These formerly enslaved workers and their families were among the free Black people living in the North and the South during later years of slavery.

But the opportunity for earning freedom did not last long. Wealthy landowners soon saw that they could make more money by keeping the Africans enslaved for life. New laws made it more difficult to free Black people and increased the punishment for enslaved workers who escaped.

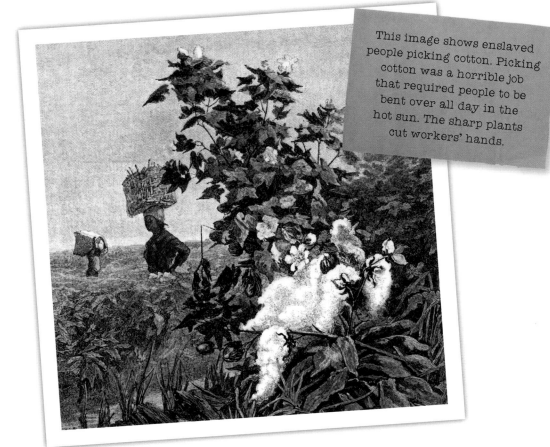

This image shows enslaved people picking cotton. Picking cotton was a horrible job that required people to be bent over all day in the hot sun. The sharp plants cut workers' hands.

Slavery continued even after Thomas Jefferson wrote the Declaration of Independence in 1776. It stated that "all men are created equal." Both Jefferson and George Washington owned slaves, despite the fact that each of them had mixed feelings about slavery.

Before the North American colonies declared and won their independence from England in the late 1770s, slavery existed in every colony. Enslaved people worked in shops in the North and on **plantations** in the South. After the Revolutionary War, some states in the North **abolished** slavery. People reasoned that to truly believe in freedom, they could not allow slavery to exist in their states. Many people also saw that slave labor, especially in the cities, was not much cheaper than hiring workers.

The majority of the people in the South had a different view. They refused to give up slavery. The disagreement between the North and the South almost split the new nation in two. Northerners avoided a break by allowing slavery into the **Constitution**. Although the Constitution does not mention slaves directly, it recognizes them indirectly by saying that only three-fifths of non-free persons would be included in the population count. More than 70 years later, the disagreement that led to this compromise helped spark the nation's Civil War.

Abolishing slavery in parts of the North created large populations of free Black people in those states. Free Black workers did not have the same rights as whites, but they had more rights than enslaved workers. Many free Black people in the North used their freedom to help enslaved workers escape.

Slavery expanded when Eli Whitney invented the cotton gin in 1793. The cotton gin meant cotton could be processed much more quickly. More enslaved workers were purchased to keep up with the demand.

Enslaved people shown using Eli Whitney's cotton gin.

LIFE OF AN ENSLAVED WORKER

For many Black people, life in the New World began on the auction block. The auction block was a place, often in the center of town, where cows, horses, and enslaved men, women, and children were bought and sold. Most enslavers were looking for workers who were strong. These people could work hard for long hours,

Enslaved people being sold at an auction in New Orleans.

plowing the land and harvesting crops such as corn, tobacco, and cotton. The buyers looked over the naked and chained new arrivals. They checked their teeth as if the enslaved people were horses. To enslavers, African people were less than human. They were little more than animals bought to perform certain tasks.

An enslaved mother and daughter are sold on the auction block. Family members were often separated.

Many enslavers used cruelty to force their workers to do jobs. Enslaved people could be whipped for not working quickly enough, for not getting out to the fields by dawn, or for almost anything else. Owners of larger farms often hired an **overseer** to ensure the enslaved people worked hard, did not rebel, and did not run away. Many overseers were known for being exceptionally cruel.

Frederick Douglass, an **abolitionist** and **fugitive** slave, described his overseer: "Mr. Severe was rightly named; he was a cruel man. I have seen him whip a woman, causing the blood to run half an hour at a time; and this too, in the midst of her crying children pleading for their mother's release."

The whips used for punishment were often several feet long and made of stiff cowhide. A single stroke of the whip could draw blood. Several strokes could make a person unconscious from the pain or cause death.

Enslaved house workers often had better living conditions and shorter working hours than field hands. Some enslavers eventually freed their house servants.

Enslavers often separated families. Children were taken from their parents. Husbands could be sold away from their wives, and siblings could be separated. Douglass wrote, "I never saw my mother, to know her as such, more than four or five times in my life. . . . She died when I was about seven years old, on one of my master's farms, near Lee's Mill. I was not allowed to be present during her illness, at her death, or burial. She was gone long before I knew anything about it."

Children of slaves were expected to start working at age five.

It was illegal to teach an enslaved person to read. Enslavers sometimes disobeyed this law, but most enslaved workers were not given the chance to learn. Enslavers wanted to keep their workers completely dependent on them. How far could an escaped slave run without knowing how to read? Enslaved children without parents were dependent on their white enslavers, no matter how cruel they were. Enslaved workers were less likely to run away or kill their enslavers if they depended on them.

Peter was an enslaved man who escaped. This 1863 photo shows the scars from his overseer's whip.

While enslaved workers were housed and fed, they rarely had enough to eat—perhaps a pint (.47 l) of rice or grain and less than a pound (.45 kg) of meat for an entire week. Often the food was rotten. Workers were sheltered in structures that looked more like horse barns than houses. The rough boards did not keep the wind out or the heat in. Instead of beds, the workers slept on narrow boards or a dirt floor. Nothing in the workers' lives belonged to them—not their clothes, their homes, their children, their work, or even their bodies. Enslavers regularly took advantage of their female slaves because no laws protected the women from rape.

Most enslaved workers knew little about their personal history. As Frederick Douglass wrote, "By far the larger part of the slaves know as little of their ages as horses know of theirs, and it is the wish of most masters within my knowledge to keep their slaves thus ignorant."

Even when not working, enslaved people had little freedom. They were not allowed to leave the plantation without permission. They could not meet in groups, even to talk about the weather. They could not buy or sell goods or hire themselves out to do a job. They were not allowed to have guns. They could not beat drums. Almost any white person could whip or beat an enslaved person for practically any reason. Enslaved Black people had no legal protection from any white person on or off the farm where they worked.

Captured Africans experienced terrible conditions when they were brought across the Atlantic. Many lawmakers were aware of this. In 1808, the U.S. government made it illegal to bring slaves into the country, but the law did not stop people from buying and selling enslaved people who were already here. And **smugglers** still forced captured Africans to America illegally, although the new law did reduce the number.

Chapter Four

RESISTANCE

Many enslavers lived in fear that their workers would rebel or fight back. Newspapers regularly reported instances of enslaved people poisoning or stabbing their owners. Some captives injured themselves so they could not work. Others killed themselves to end a lifetime of slavery.

Other workers organized in groups to rise up against their enslavers. Gabriel Prosser led a famous **revolt** in 1800. More than 1,000 enslaved Virginia workers, led by Prosser, armed themselves and marched on Richmond. The revolt fell apart after two enslaved people reported the plan to whites. The governor of Virginia sent troops to crush the uprising. Prosser and other leaders were captured and executed.

Denmark Vesey led a similar revolt in Charlestown, South Carolina, in 1822. Vesey had bought his freedom more than 20 years earlier. For many years, he had gathered weapons and supporters with the aim of ending slavery in the region. An estimated 9,000 enslaved people were involved in the plot, but word reached the local authorities. Before Vesey's revolt could begin, 139 Black people were arrested. Forty-seven Black people were executed. Four whites went to prison for helping with the revolt.

Nat Turner, an enslaved worker and a preacher, led the most effective revolt in the United States. In 1831, Turner and other enslaved workers joined together and killed approximately 60 whites in Southampton, Virginia. State and federal troops eventually stopped Turner's small army. Turner escaped but was later captured and executed. His revolt encouraged many Black people to fight for their freedom.

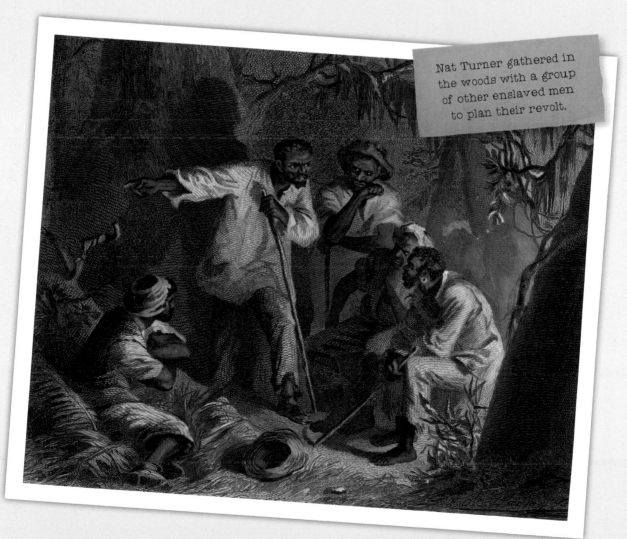

Nat Turner gathered in the woods with a group of other enslaved men to plan their revolt.

This portrait of Harriet Tubman is thought to have been taken in the 1860s. After escaping slavery, Tubman became a conductor on the Underground Railroad.

Every year, thousands of enslaved people ran away to freedom. Some escaped alone, but many others had help from the **Underground Railroad**. The Underground Railroad was not an actual railroad, but a group of people in both the North and the South who helped Black people escape slavery. They gave the fugitives food and shelter during the long journey north. Some "conductors" on the Underground Railroad went with the fugitives, directing them to safety. The most famous conductor was Harriet Tubman. She escaped slavery herself as a young woman but returned to the South many times to help other enslaved people escape.

Escaping slavery was not easy. The fugitives had to travel hundreds of miles on foot. They moved by night and hid by day, often disguising themselves. Most importantly, they had to avoid patrols and bounty hunters. Patrols were groups of armed whites who regularly traveled an area, looking for escaped Black workers. Bounty hunters chased and caught fugitives to collect a reward for their return.

Many women took a special interest in abolishing slavery. Women such as Sojourner Truth, Lucretia Mott, and Lydia Marie Child believed a nation that enslaved Black people would never fully respect the rights of women.

Enslaved people escape on foot and on horseback with the help of the Underground Railroad.

Chapter Five

SLAVERY'S END

By the 1830s, enslaved Black people had become a major workforce. In many parts of the South, enslaved Black people far outnumbered white people. As slavery grew, so did opposition to it. How could a nation founded on "life, liberty, and the pursuit of happiness" deny even the most basic freedoms to millions of human beings?

Northerners, both Black and white, spoke out more and more against slavery. People who opposed slavery called themselves abolitionists because they wanted to abolish, or end, slavery.

This photo from 1862 shows enslaved people on the Cassina Point plantation in South Carolina.

The *Liberator*, published by William Lloyd Garrison, was one of several antislavery newspapers that were printed in the North.

Several antislavery newspapers sprang up in the North. The most famous was called the *Liberator*. It appeared in January of 1831. The editor, a white man named William Lloyd Garrison, became one of the nation's most outspoken critics of slavery. Two years before the *Liberator* first appeared, a free Black man named David Walker printed a powerful essay. He declared that Black people had the right to resist slavery—with force, if necessary. His powerful words terrified many whites and challenged enslaved Black people to win their freedom.

Dozens of abolitionists formed groups, wrote letters to the government, and gave lectures condemning slavery. Perhaps the greatest among them was Frederick Douglass. While enslaved in the South, Douglass learned to read. He escaped slavery as a young man and became the nation's most forceful antislavery speaker and writer.

In 1845, Frederick Douglass published his own story, *Narrative of the Life of Frederick Douglass, An American Slave*. The book became a best-seller and now is considered an American classic.

Douglass eventually created his own antislavery newspaper called the *North Star*. He chose the name because fugitives from slavery often used the North Star to guide them at night.

Douglass and other abolitionists convinced many Northerners to oppose slavery. As antislavery beliefs grew, the nation became more and more divided.

In the mid-1800s, the United States was still expanding. Most Southerners wanted slavery to be allowed in the new territories. Most Northerners did not. Disagreement in the territories became so strong that citizens in the North and South began to fight one another.

Disagreement was serious in the U.S. Congress as well. Representatives and senators from the South threatened to withdraw their states from the **Union** if they were not allowed to bring slavery into the new territories. They believed that individual states should be able to decide whether or not slavery should be allowed. Northerners believed the federal government should decide. The United States faced a major crisis. If Southern states left the Union, or **seceded**, the government would have to use force to keep the nation united.

Frederick Douglass, a well-known abolitionist, spoke out against slavery in his speeches and writings.

This 1864 photo shows the 4th U.S. Colored Infantry regiment. This unit of free and formerly enslaved Black men fought for the Union.

The disagreement between the North and South helped drive the United States toward a civil war. Abraham Lincoln was elected president in 1860. Much of the South believed that Lincoln was an abolitionist who wanted to destroy slavery. Several Southern states decided to secede and form their own country. When Southern troops attacked a U.S. fort on April 12, 1861, Union troops fought back. The U.S. Civil War had begun.

At the start of the war, slavery was not the main issue for the federal government. President Lincoln knew that many Northerners would not fight a war to free slaves, but they would fight to preserve the Union. Southerners said they were fighting for individual states' rights. Even so, the war could decide the future of slavery.

At first, the Union army turned away Black volunteers. Even though many Northerners opposed slavery, they still had racist beliefs. But after Union troops lost battle after battle to the South, the North decided to allow Black soldiers to join the Union army. Black people knew that this was their time to fight for freedom. Thousands of free Black people joined the army, and thousands more escaped slavery to join as well.

General Robert E. Lee surrendered his Southern army to General Ulysses S. Grant on April 9, 1865. The North won the war, but President Lincoln did not live to see the end of slavery. Lincoln was assassinated on April 14, 1865, months before the Thirteenth Amendment became law.

Black troops were not treated as equals. They received lower pay and poor equipment. At first, they were not even allowed to fight in battles. But the South kept beating the North in battles, and the Union army needed more troops. Eventually, the Union army treated its Black troops better.

Although the U.S. Civil War was fought for a number of reasons, it finally led to the end of slavery. In January of 1863, President Lincoln issued the Emancipation Proclamation, which freed slaves in all rebel states. Lincoln did not have the power to enforce the order at that time, but the act itself helped the North in its fight.

Black troops fought bravely in many battles, helping the North win the Civil War. They fought to keep the nation together, but they also fought for freedom—for themselves and for others. People knew that if the South won the war, slavery would continue. When the North won in 1865, the end of slavery was in sight.

Freed slaves celebrate the abolition of slavery.

Slavery did not end right away, however. The U.S. Congress had to pass **amendments** to the Constitution to put an end to slavery for good. In 1865, the Thirteenth Amendment made slavery illegal. In 1868, the Fourteenth Amendment made all former slaves citizens, just like anyone else born in the United States. The Fifteenth Amendment gave Black men the right to vote in 1870. (Women of all races did not win the right to vote in the United States until 1920, with the passing of the Nineteenth Amendment.)

The end of slavery did not mean the end of racism. The government did not always enforce these new amendments to the Constitution. The end of slavery was the beginning of another long journey—the struggle to bring equal treatment to all people. That journey continues today.

Slavery was a terrible institution that destroyed the lives of many people. Millions of people endured slavery or fought to end it. Learning about their struggles can help us appreciate the value of freedom.

Slavery began thousands of years ago and took place in many different countries. Slavery began in North America in the 1600s and lasted more than two centuries.

What were the assumptions and biases that slavery was built on?

William Lloyd Garrison, a white man, was an outspoken critic of slavery.

Is it important for white people to stand with Black people in their fight for freedom and equality? Why or why not?

TIME LINE

1500-1699

1501
Europeans begin transporting enslaved Africans to the Western Hemisphere to replace Native American slaves.

1619
The first enslaved Africans land in North America at the settlement of Jamestown.

1700-1799

1776
The United States declares its independence from England. Thomas Jefferson writes in the Declaration of Independence that "all men are created equal."

1787
The U.S. Constitution allows slavery to exist in the new nation.

1800-1829

1800
Gabriel Prosser leads a large but unsuccessful revolt of enslaved workers in Virginia.

1808
A new law makes it illegal to bring slaves to the United States from Africa.

1822
Denmark Vesey, a free Black man, plots a large revolt of enslaved workers in South Carolina. Whites discover the plot, and the revolt never takes place.

Black people endured hundreds years of slavery in America.
How does that affect the life of a Black person today?

The United States was built on the free labor of enslaved Black workers.
As a result of this, many white families have enormous wealth when compared
to Black families. Some people think whites should pay families of formerly
enslaved workers to account for their ancestor's free labor.
What do you think?

1830-1859

1831
William Lloyd Garrison, a white abolitionist, founds an antislavery newspaper called the *Liberator*. In August, Nat Turner leads a Virginia rebellion in which about 60 whites are killed. Turner and his men are eventually captured and executed.

1847
Frederick Douglass, a Black abolitionist and fugitive slave, starts an antislavery newspaper called the *North Star*.

1860-1879

1860
Abraham Lincoln is elected president of the United States. Southerners believe he is an abolitionist who will end slavery.

1861
Many Southern states secede from the United States. This action leads to the U.S. Civil War, which begins on April 12.

1863
Abraham Lincoln issues the Emancipation Proclamation.

1865
The North defeats the South in the Civil War, which ends in April. The Thirteenth Amendment to the U.S. Constitution declares slavery to be illegal in December.

1868
The Fourteenth Amendment to the Constitution grants full citizenship to all formerly enslaved people.

1870
The Fifteenth Amendment guarantees Black men the right to vote.

abolished (uh-BOL-ishd)
Abolished means putting an end to something officially. In the United States, slavery was finally abolished after the end of the Civil War, with the passage of the Thirteenth Amendment.

abolitionist (ab-uh-LISH-uh-nist)
An abolitionist was someone who worked to abolish slavery before the Civil War. Frederick Douglass was a famous abolitionist.

amendments (uh-MEND-munts)
Amendments are changes that are made to a law or legal document. Congress had to pass amendments to the Constitution to end slavery.

bondage (BON-dij)
People who are kept in bondage are held against their will. Enslaved Africans were held in bondage.

Constitution (kon-stuh-TOO-shun)
The Constitution is the written document containing the principles by which the United States is governed. The Constitution had to be amended to outlaw slavery.

fugitive (FYOO-juh-tiv)
Someone who is running away, especially from the law, is a fugitive. An enslaved worker who escaped from slavery was a fugitive.

inhumane (in-hyoo-MAYN)
Inhumane means cruel and brutal. Treatment of slaves was often inhumane.

overseer (OH-vur-see-ur)
An overseer is a person who supervises others as they work. On plantations, an overseer supervised the slaves.

plantations (plan-TAY-shuns)
Plantations are large farms, often in the South. Many slaves were forced to work on plantations.

prejudice (PREJ-uh-diss)
Prejudice means a negative feeling or opinion about someone without just cause. Even after slavery ended, prejudice about race continued.

racism (RAY-sih-zum)
The belief that one race is superior to another is called racism. Racism remained a problem even after slavery had ended.

revolt (rih-VOLT)
A revolt is a rebellion against a government or an authority. Nat Turner led a famous revolt in Virginia.

secede (sih-SEED)
To secede is to formally withdraw from an organization, often to form another organization. At the start of the U.S. Civil War, Southern states decided to secede from the United States to form their own nation.

smugglers (SMUG-lerz)
Smugglers are people who bring goods into a country illegally. Bringing slaves into the United States eventually became illegal, but smugglers still brought them in.

Underground Railroad (UN-der-grownd RAYL-rohd)
The Underground Railroad was a group of people who helped Black people escape slavery before the U.S. Civil War. Many people worked hard to make the Underground Railroad a success.

Union (YOON-yuhn)
Union is another way of referring to the United States of America. The Union won the U.S. Civil War.

BOOKS

Alexander, Richard. *The Transatlantic Slave Trade: The Forced Migration of Africans to America.* New York, NY: PowerKids Press, 2016.

Asim, Jabari. *A Child's Introduction to African American History: The Experiences, People, and Events That Shaped Our Country.* New York, NY: Black Dog & Leventhal, 2018.

Lester, Julius. *From Slave Ship to Freedom Road.* New York, NY: Puffin Books, 2000.

McDonough, Yona Zeldis. *What Was the Underground Railroad?* New York, NY: Grosset & Dunlap, 2013.

Nelson, Kadir. *Heart and Soul: The Story of America and African Americans.* Solon, OH: Findaway World, 2019.

Ransome, James E. *The Bell Rang.* New York, NY: Atheneum. 2019.

WEBSITES

Visit our website for links about Slavery:

childsworld.com/links

Note to Parents, Teachers, and Librarians: We routinely verify our Web links to make sure they are safe, active sites—so encourage your readers to check them out!